The United States Army War College

The United States Army War College (USAWC) educates and develops leaders for service at the strategic level while advancing knowledge in the global application of Landpower. The purpose of the USAWC is to produce graduates who are skilled critical thinkers and complex problem solvers. Concurrently, it is the USAWC's duty to the U.S. Army to also act as a "think factory" for commanders and civilian leaders at the strategic level worldwide and routinely engage in discourse and debate concerning the role of ground forces in achieving national security objectives.

The Carlisle Scholars Program

The Carlisle Scholars Program (CSP) seeks to educate select USAWC students through innovative, purpose-driven projects undertaken in partnership with the strategic-level defense analysis and decision making communities. CSP scholars "learn by doing," as they gain a practical understanding of strategy and policy development via direct participation in important debates alongside working analysts and defense stakeholders. CSP students are provided with enhanced opportunities to substantively examine and influence important national security issues through collaborative relationships with senior government decision makers and leading policy experts. With support of USAWC faculty, scholars pursue both individual and collaborative research and writing initiatives. In every instance, the individual student's charter is to gain new understanding of a critical issue and translate that understanding either into a more thorough appreciation of the current and future decision making context or a set of actionable recommendations for senior leaders. In the end, CSP aims to build and maintain a lasting dialogue between USAWC, its faculty, its students, and the wider national security analysis and decision making communities.

Disclaimer

This final report of the Russia wargame hosted April 15 and 16, 2015, is produced under the purview of the United States Army War College to foster dialogue of topics with strategic ramifications.

The ideas and viewpoints advanced in this publication are those of the authors and do not necessarily reflect the official policy or position of the institution, the Department of Defense, or any other department or agency of the United States Government.

Authors, Editor, and Contributors

Report Authors

COL Gregory K. Anderson, U.S. Army

COL Gert-Jan Kooij, Royal Netherlands Army

LTC Karen L.T. Briggman, U.S. Army

LTC Joseph E. Hilbert, U.S. Army

Lt Col Christopher T. Lay, U.S. Air Force

Dr. James C. McNaughton, Department of the Army Civilian

Report Editor

Dr. John R. Deni, Strategic Studies Institute

Contributors

Center for Strategic Leadership and Development (CSLD)

Strategic Studies Institute (SSI)

Table of Contents

Acknowledgements

The authors wish to thank the following individuals for their participation in the wargame. Their participation should not imply endorsement or concurrence by either them personally or by their respective organizations.

Mr. Spiro Ballas, U.S. Department of State

Dr. Jorge Benitez, Atlantic Council

COL Robert Drozd, Polish Army, International Fellow, U.S. Army War College

Mr. Stewart Eales, U.S. Department of State Fellow, U.S. Army War College

COL Bob Hamilton, U.S. Army War College

Mr. Rick Hoehne, U.S. Defense Intelligence Agency Fellow, U.S. Army War College

COL Pat Huston, U.S. Army War College

CW5 Roger Jacobs, U.S. Army Europe

LTC Arturas Jasinskas, Lithuanian Army, International Fellow, U.S. Army War College

Mr. Steven Keil, The German Marshall Fund of the United States

LTC Mike Kimberly, Supreme Headquarters Allied Powers Europe

LTC David Kynch, U.S. Army War College

COL Chris Lackovic, U.S. Army War College

Dr. Jeff Mankoff, Center for Security and International Studies

Dr. Craig Nation, U.S. Army War College

Dr. Karl Qualls, Dickinson College

Mr. Stephen de Spiegeleire, The Hague Center for Security Studies

Dr. Marybeth Ulrich, U.S. Army War College

Dr. Sufian Zhemukhov, George Washington University

Additionally, the authors would like to thank the numerous U.S. Army War College students, international fellows, and faculty who participated as wargame observers and advisors.

Executive Summary

Russian aggression in 2014 caught U.S. policy and strategy off guard, forcing reactive measures and reevaluation of the U.S. approach toward Russia. Moscow employed nonlinear methodologies and operated just beneath traditional thresholds of conflict to take full advantage of U.S. and NATO policy and process limitations. In light of this strategic problem, the U.S. Army War College (US-AWC), conducted a wargame that revealed four key considerations for future policy and strategy.

- ## The U.S. must shift from a mostly cooperative approach towards Russia to one that recognizes the competitive nature of Moscow

  Moscow consistently pursues the development of frozen conflicts, exclusionary bi-lateral relationships, "sweetheart" and opaque economic deals, and proxy forces willing to promote Russian interests, all in an effort to 'win' against the West. Meanwhile, current U.S. policy describes Russia as both a competitor and a cooperative partner. In reality it is clear that the U.S. and Russian systems are inherently competitive, especially regarding Russia's "near abroad," NATO, Asia, and the Arctic. A clear U.S. policy that illuminates the competitive nature of the two systems is a necessary step towards regaining the strategic initiative.

- ## U.S. policy must clearly articulate its position toward Russia, Eastern Europe, and Ukraine

  U.S. lack of clarity and prioritization toward Russia, Eastern Europe, and Ukraine creates hesitancy and risk aversion, and limits innovation on both sides of the Atlantic. The United States must develop a coherent, unified policy toward Russia, one that avoids creating disunity within the transatlantic community.

  Differences in how the United States and Europe view the incorporation of Russia into a European security architecture are fundamental and will continue to create wedges in the transatlantic community that Moscow will seek to exploit.

  To strengthen deterrence and reassurance, the United States should consistently reiterate its Article 5 obligations. Meanwhile, Washington must also clarify U.S. interests in the Ukraine crisis, otherwise it is likely to continue causing confusion among European allies.

• U.S. policy must challenge Russia in the competition of ideas and influence

Russia emphasizes information operations as central to its strategy. The United States advocates the power and influence of a truthful message, but approaches the issue more defensively and incoherently. The United States must undertake a more robust information campaign.

• U.S. policy must account for the two national election cycles in 2016 and 2018

President Putin needs a political "win" before 2017 to ensure success in the 2018 Russian elections. What is unknown is what actions he will take to achieve that "win" and how he may use the U.S. election cycle as an opportunity. The United States must be pro-active in shaping the environment prior to Putin taking the initiative.

Introduction

The reemergence of Russian aggression in 2014 forced an immediate review and evaluation of U.S. policy and strategy toward Europe and Russia. Russian nonlinear approaches, often operating just beneath traditional thresholds of conflict, exploited weaknesses of longstanding U.S. and NATO policy constructs, exposing gaps and seams that now require reexamination. Trends within the strategic environment indicate that the nature of the U.S.-Russian relationship is likely to remain competitive, thus requiring a critical look at current assumptions and a comprehensive reexamination of Western thinking about Russia.

In support of that reexamination, in October 2014, a team of six students from the CSP at the USAWC began a six-month project to assess the driving factors behind Russian foreign and security policy, in order to better anticipate future behavior. The project was grounded in systems thinking and aimed at building a strategic-level system design of Russia as a point of departure for research, analysis, collaboration, and experimentation. The CSP team created a visualization and formal paper describing what it came to term "the Russian System," culminating in a strategic-level wargame to test key hypotheses and expand collaborative learning. This report provides some insights into the broader project, but is more focused on the results of the wargame and how those results can inform future thinking about U.S.-Russian relations.

Methodology

Systems thinking is a subcategory of critical thinking and an appropriate tool for addressing complex, strategic-level problems. This project attempted to see Russia holistically, properly arranging Russian actors and relationships and defining the environmental, historical, and cultural forces behind observed system behavior and patterns. The overarching idea behind this method, is that once one can fully visualize a system and begin to understand that system's logic, one can better anticipate future behavior, identify second and third order effects, accurately conceptualize risk, and potentially influence strategic outcomes. Here is a synopsis of the system design method to learning that produced the team's understanding of the Russian System:

1) **Initial Research** – The team conducted intensive research into Russian history, economy, politics, and military reform. Additionally, the team reviewed current news reports, field reports, and commentary by Russia experts across multiple disciplines. This created the foundation to begin initial system design.

2) **Brainstorming and Synthesis** – The team identified the array of actors, relationships, and forces that contribute to Russian behavior. This established the framework for the Russian System, but fell short in fully explaining causal relationships. Assumptions and hypotheses generated from these sessions drove additional research and review.

3) **Follow-on Research** – The team conducted another research effort dedicated to accumulating more data to support, or disprove, ideas discussed during initial system synthesis.

4) **Visualization of the Russian System** – As additional data and analytical refinement strengthened the team's understanding of the array of actors and forces, the next step was to create a visualization of the system to guide further analysis.

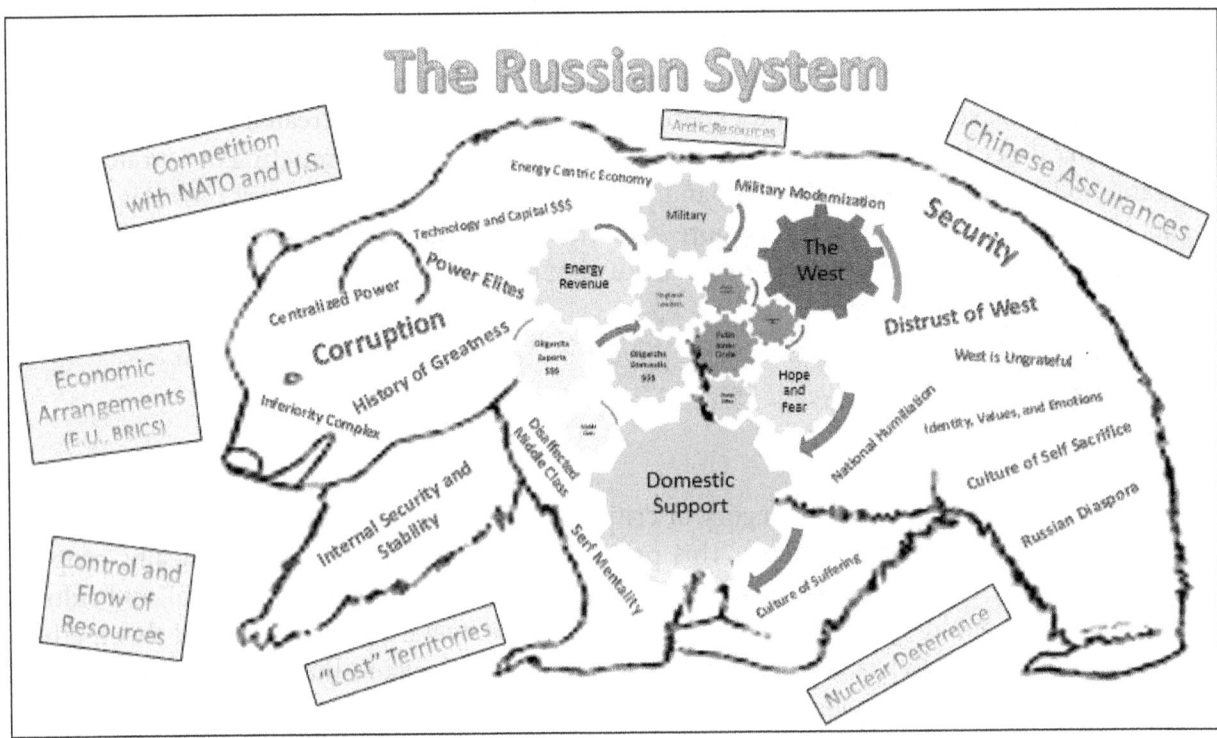

Figure 1: Visualization of the Russian System

5) **Collaborative Learning and System Reframe** – Over the next three months, the team engaged think tanks, Department of Defense entities, academic institutions, and international organizations to discuss and critique the conceptualization of the Russian System. These discussions resulted in further refinement of the system model and the causal relationships that underpin it.

6) **Wargame and System Testing** – On 15 and 16 April 2015, the U.S. Army War College hosted a strategic level wargame designed to test the ideas behind the Russia System and act as a venue for thought experimentation, synthesis of perspectives, and competitive heuristics related to the nature of U.S.-Russian relations. The overarching objective of the effort was to assess the implications for the U.S. military of various potential future scenarios.

Wargame Design

The U.S. Army War College designed the wargame to be a semi-competitive, heuristic exercise to test and improve understanding of the Russia System while facilitating a more rigorous assessment of the likely future directions of U.S.-Russian relations through introduction of dynamic uncertainty, differing perspectives, multiple domains, and analysis of all elements of national power. In order to achieve these objectives, participants were divided into three teams – a Russia Team, a U.S. Team, and a 'White Cell' Team.

The Russia Team was comprised of academics, think tank experts, State Department personnel, and Department of Defense experts on Russia. The Russia team included a wide range of perspectives, including "Kremlinologists" and Russian historians, native Russian-speaking journalists, and inter-agency experts on current Russian affairs. The Russia Team played the role of Putin's inner circle in the Kremlin and was charged with seeking ways to expand and improve Russian standing and influence, while maintaining Putin's grip on political power.

The U.S. Team was comprised of current NATO planners, Russia scholars, and European security policy experts from multiple think tanks, the State Department, academia, and the U.S. military. The U.S. Team played the role of U.S. policy makers in Washington, DC and were required to carefully consider EU, NATO, and individual European national perspectives throughout the wargame. Their goal was to create policy and strategy designed to maintain a stable, secure, and prosperous Europe in accordance with National Security Strategy objectives.

The White Team was comprised predominantly of Army War College students, faculty, and international fellows from NATO countries and Eastern European Partners. The role of the White Team was to assess U.S. and Russian policy choices, and provide insights from the represented national perspectives.

The wargame consisted of several possible future scenarios involving the United States and Russia. The scenarios were designed to challenge certain elements of the Russian System in a progressively more rigorous fashion. The scenarios were presented in a six-turn sequence, with each turn comprised of a period for Russia and U.S. team deliberation, policy implementation, and then reactive counter-moves. Meanwhile, the White Team also deliberated each turn, and offered analysis and evaluation of decisions by the Russia and U.S. teams. The turns were as follows:

1) The status quo continues for an indefinite period with little significant change

2) Europe moves rapidly towards energy independence from Russia

3) Expansion of the conflict in Eastern Ukraine and a regional miscalculation

4) A nationalist uprising within Russia and incident within the Baltic States

5) Putin is removed from power and Russia must stabilize its situation

6) Getting beyond a constant state of crisis

Turn 1: Continuation of Status Quo

The first session tasked each team with examining current policies and strategies, and to assess the implications of the status quo persisting for some period of time. The White Team focused its efforts on providing a Euro-centric critique of current Russia and U.S. policy.

The Russia Team looked carefully at the forces that are driving current Russian behavior and policy. Although there was not complete consensus on what Russia's objectives are, there was general agreement on several policy and strategy related issues. Key points discussed during this turn included the following:

> "Russia appears to seek global relevance."

- Does Putin have a grand strategy?
  - Perhaps he does not, and is instead improvising and adjusting as he navigates Russia through the strategic environment.
  - On the other hand, perhaps the strategic aim for Putin and his trusted circle is the maintenance, preservation, and perpetuation of the current system of power and wealth distribution with Russia.
  - From another perspective, Putin's strategy appears focused on restoring Russian greatness and prestige in the eyes of Russians and the international community.
- Russian behavior appears to be driven by a feeling of constraint. The United States and the greater West are typically viewed as interfering with Russian desires, creating conditions for a competitive relationship.
  - Ironically though, Russians may be willing to pardon or tolerate Western interference in exchange for capital investment.
- Russia appears to seek global relevance. Investment in global reach technologies and capabilities demonstrates that Russia is not content to confine its influence to the 'near abroad' and other surrounding territories.
- Russians appear somewhat hesitant to use overt military action to achieve policy aims. In some cases, they seem more comfortable cloaking their military actions with other events, and fully integrating military force with other elements of na

- tional power. They also seem keenly aware of how far they can push the United States and the North Atlantic Treaty Organization (NATO) without provoking an unintended conflict.

- Putin appears to find great utility in creating 'frozen conflicts', perhaps as a means of providing Russia with tools to barter, negotiate, or rapidly escalate or deescalate.

Meanwhile, the U.S. Team was in agreement that current U.S. policy needs adjustment in order to recognize U.S.-Russian strategic competition. Following additional deliberation, the U.S. Team concluded that the status quo would not suffice in safeguarding American or Western interests at a reasonable cost. Hence, the U.S. Team discussed how the status quo could be strengthened:

- And should continue to deter any Russian efforts to destabilize U.S. allies and European partners, and the United States should continue to affirm the importance of sovereignty and the rules of the international system.

- The United States should initiate a discussion within NATO clarifying the meaning of Article 5 in an era of emerging security issues, including cyber conflict, hybrid warfare, and energy security.

- The United States should continue to seek areas of cooperation with Russia on a range of regional and global issues. Nonetheless, a return to business as usual – perhaps through another 'reset' with Russia – is not possible in the short term.

- The United States should give higher strategic priority to Europe and consider stationing additional military forces in strategic locations within the region.

After the Russia and U.S. teams presented their assessments, the White Team – comprised primarily of Europeans – shared the results of their analysis:

- Continuation of the status quo perpetuates what many in Europe perceive as a lack of clarity, prioritization, and strength in U.S. policy.

- The status quo risks allowing economic and social conditions in Ukraine to worsen in the near to mid-term.

- Subsequently, the status quo may facilitate or promote Russian advantages in narrative and strategic initiative.

- Current information and influence operations by the United States are ineffective.

- The current Article 5 construct may not be sufficient given information and cyber infractions against NATO allies. The United States should lead this discussion for it to resonate among the 28 member nations.

- Current U.S. and Western policies may not sufficiently appreciate Russia's perceptions of *honor* and *power*. Failure to account for Russian perceptions of these and related concepts may reinforce Putin's narrative and his appeal within Russia.

- The United States should continue its efforts at building partner capacity -- strengthening NATO and the European Union (EU) will increase the role of European partners and will reduce strategic costs in the long term.

Turn 2: Europe Moves Rapidly Towards Energy Independence from Russia

In this scenario, the teams explored the implications of a more energy independent Europe within the next five years. This scenario assumed that Russian attempts to fracture NATO through energy leverage deals had backfired and a unified Europe reacted by seeking alternative energy sources. Consequently, the United States and Europe started to earnestly develop the necessary infrastructure and diversification to insure their energy needs without fear of Russian manipulation or leverage.

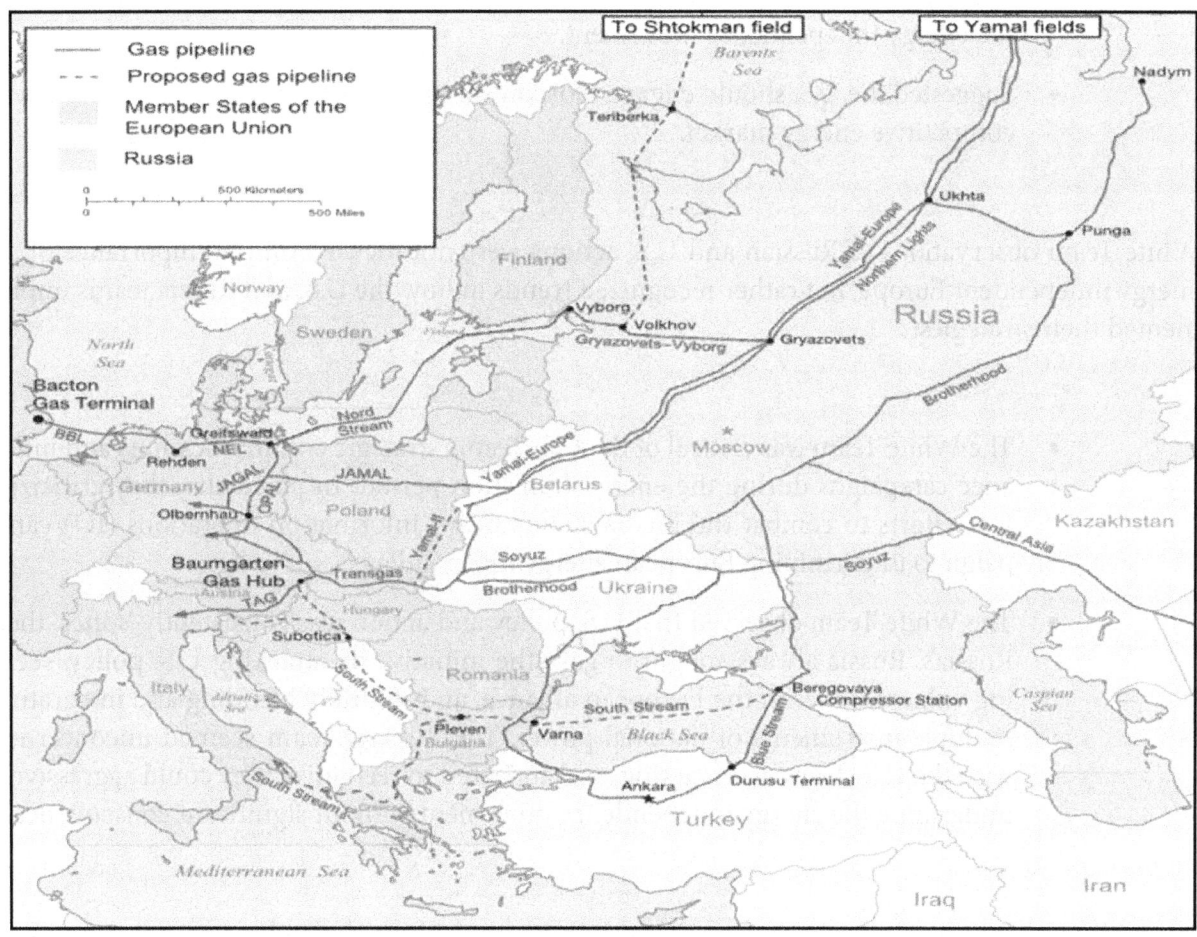

Figure 2: Russian Gas Pipelines

The Russia Team sought to take advantage of their short-term advantages in the energy market and extract as much capital as possible from the West, largely as a means of safeguarding Russia's fiscal situation and forestalling domestic political tensions that could arise in the wake of

- Supported Russia's desires to sell energy to Europe, but wanted to ensure the arrangement somehow precluded Russian 'bullying' of energy importing nations in Europe.

- Proposed investment of public and private funds into infrastructure and technology to improve storage and security of hydrocarbons, to include investment in Ukrainian energy infrastructure to increase capacity.

- Sought to prepare the EU and NATO for Russian attempts to undermine energy transformation, including Russian pressure on Ukraine, launching cyber-attacks targeting key energy transit nodes in the public and private sectors, and seeking to influence political parties and NGOs in Eastern and Central Europe to not support the energy independence movement.

- Suggested the U.S. should engage Moscow on the benefits to Russia of a more open, competitive energy market.

White Team observations of Russian and U.S. actions were not focused on the importance of an energy independent Europe, but rather recognized trends in how the U.S. and Russia teams implemented their strategies:

- The White Team was critical of the U.S. Team's strategic communications and influence campaigns during the energy transition period. In particular, they criticized U.S. efforts to combat the Russia Team's heavy information operations (IO) campaign to undermining European energy independence.

- The White Team observed that U.S. policy and action was consistently 'softer' than Russia's. Russia always sought to gain the initiative by attacking U.S. policy, seeking vulnerabilities in the European alliance, and skillfully blending and integrating multiple instruments of national power. The Russian Team seemed unconcerned with the U.S. Team overreacting, and appeared to recognize they could aggressively undermine the energy independence movement without significant consequence.

This scenario validated the idea that a Europe less energy dependent on Russia is more secure. However, total energy independence from Russia did not appear to be in either team's interests. Rather, any concerted attempt towards energy independence will force a significant Russian response. Although concerned with the idea of an energy independent Europe, Moscow is likely to remain confident that it has the time and leverage to undermine these efforts. Both the U.S. and Russia teams identified common interests in ensuring continued energy investments, economic diversification, and healthy economic competition.

higher unemployment and slower economic growth. The question of European energy independence was a serious matter for the Russia Team as they sought to undermine Western policies aimed at European energy diversification. Nevertheless, the desire for increased security competition with the West was limited. The Russia Team instead offered a rational, pragmatic, and proactive approach, which included the following:

- Undermining European plans through the pursuit of "sweetheart" deals with energy vulnerable states.

- Preserving long term access to energy revenue through demand diversification into Africa, China, and India.

- Increasing energy prices in the short term to take advantage of current European energy dependence and extract as much capital as possible, and subsequently investing these energy windfalls into diversification, expansion, and modernization of energy sectors.

- Leveraging Moscow's relationship with Germany to undermine European plans for energy independence.

- Accelerating attempts to improve effectiveness in combating corruption as a means to make the Russian budget and economy more resilient and less wasteful.

- Continuing to bear in mind the impact of reduced government revenues on the 2018 Russian national elections.

The U.S. Team responded to this scenario by acknowledging the need for a global energy market that works better for all suppliers and consumers. While the team was not able to more fully develop what defined this market, they did note that it would include a more resilient and efficient liquefied natural gas (LNG) market and sought a market in which natural gas was no longer. More broadly though, the key concern was maintaining European unity. The U.S. Team emphasized the need to demonstrate support for European energy needs, while ensuring that all stakeholders understood the security consequences of energy dependence on Russia. In summary, the U.S. Team:

The United States must help to preclude "Russian 'bullying' of energy importing nations in Europe"

Turn 3: Ukraine Conflict Expands / Potential for a Regional Miscalculation Increases

One of the more likely scenarios to unfold in the coming months is a violation of the current Minsk II Agreement and subsequent expansion of the conflict within Ukraine. In this scenario, pro-Russian separatists resumed offensive combat operations in Eastern Ukraine with the goal of capturing Mariupol. Tensions between Russia and Ukraine also manifested themselves in an exchange of gunfire between Ukrainian security forces and Russian soldiers exercising within Transnistria, along Ukraine's border with Moldova. Adding to this was a bomb blast in Ukraine that caused the deaths of two U.S. soldiers involved in training Ukrainian Defense Forces. Lastly, concerned leaders in Tbilisi, following the completion of a NATO-Georgian military exercise, and in light of the expanded conflict in Ukraine, began aggressive lobbying both publically and privately for NATO to move forward with the promise of membership and issue Georgia a Membership Action Plan.

The Russia Team was unified in its support for ethnic Russians within Ukraine and was determined not to let Russian separatists fail. Despite this backing, the Russia Team was non-supportive of the attempt to capture Mariupol. The Russia Team was not concerned with establishing a land bridge to support Crimea – especially given the escalatory nature of such an operation and the difficulty of defending any such gains – and hence were content to maintain the status quo established by the Minsk II Agreement. The Russia Team was generally more interested in keeping their strategic advantages with the current 'frozen conflict' and did not wish to escalate, although they did see these events as an opportunity to discredit and disadvantage the United States. Moreover, the Russia Team had the following observations:

> *"The United States should consider designating both Ukraine and Georgia as major non-NATO allies."*

- The Minsk II Agreement seems acceptable to all parties except Ukraine.
- Russia, the United States, and Europe can afford to be patient and careful regarding Ukraine, while leaders in Kyiv attempt to make this a time-sensitive crisis.

- Moscow would likely vehemently deny any involvement in provoking events in Moldova or in the death of U.S. troops. To the contrary, Russia would be likely to blame the United States for the deaths, due to Washington's meddling in the region.

- The United States would be unlikely to allow Georgia to become a NATO member due to intra-alliance disagreements on this subject, and due to a fear of provoking Russia. Hence it would be best for Moscow to allow NATO to deny Georgia membership, and then immediately make positive overtures to establish better relations between Russia and Georgia while simultaneously discrediting the United States and NATO.

The U.S. Team saw this crisis as a chance to place a higher strategic priority on Ukraine, making it central to the core U.S. policy of deterring Russian aggression. The U.S. Team wanted to ensure it clearly communicated to both Russia and Europe the American readiness and willingness to prevent Moscow from further destabilizing the region. The U.S. Team agreed that, in light of the unfolding scenario, previous approaches had likely been too 'soft' and ambiguous, and that the United States should endeavor to communicate strength during this crisis. Other observations and assessments are as follows:

- The United States should consider designating both Ukraine and Georgia as major non-NATO allies. This was both a diplomatic symbol and an avenue for providing increase security assistance, training opportunities, and armaments to these states.

- Washington ought to promote greater NATO support in the region.

- Although underwriting Ukrainian and Georgian security in a more open, aggressive manner would cause controversy within NATO and risk feeding Russia's anti-Western narrative, the risk of inaction would likely be more dangerous.

- The United States ought to consider raising the costs to Russia for any conflict expansion, though imposing sanctions on Society for Worldwide Interbank Financial Telecommunication (SWIFT) network transactions between banks ought to be held in abeyance for the moment.

- Ukraine would likely be the best place to confront Russia and to send a clear message of intent, capability, and will.

White Team observations were focused on Russian advantages in the region and the difficulty the United States faces when trying to counter these advantages. Additionally, the White Team was quick to recognize the risks the United States incurs when pursuing actions independent of Europe and NATO:

- The United States has a greater evidentiary standard than Russia when proving intent and involvement in the region. The United States must accept a burden of proof beyond a reasonable doubt, where Russia only needs to show a degree of doubt. This dynamic plays into Russian success with ambiguous approaches and Moscow's ability to create uncertainty and doubt within the West.

- Time is one of Russia's greatest advantages – they can wait for small gains, consolidate them patiently, de-escalate tensions, and then wait and set conditions for the next opportunity. Western reactive policies play to this strength.

- Proposed American reactions as outlined by the U.S. Team would be too reactionary in their approach. Only after the deaths of U.S. soldiers, or some similar tragedy, would a stronger policy and strategy be put in place.

- The United States ought to increase diplomatic efforts with France and Germany. That solidarity, they argued, would prove formidable to Russia, though the United States must be ready to manage and overcome a European perspective that some battles cannot be won.

Overall, the notable disparity on how to approach war in Ukraine and Crimea only served to reinforce the frozen conflict within the region. The Russia Team consistently sought to develop tools to enable strategic flexibility in the absence of a long term strategy. The creation of proxies, bi-lateral relationships, "sweetheart" economic deals, and information and influence campaigns are the mechanisms that could allow Russia to take advantage of strategic opportunities or to hedge against uncertainty. This scenario showed a clear parallel between current observed Russian behavior and a Russia penchant for creating multiple options in lieu of pursuing a single, clear, long-term strategy.

Turn 4: Runaway Nationalism in Russia

Throughout the conflicts of the Putin era, Russia has 'weaponized' nationalism, using aggressive patriotic rhetoric as part of influence campaigns to motivate the Russian population at home and across the near abroad. By blaming the West and accusing NATO of threatening Russia, Putin builds and furthers anti-Western feelings and encourages a dangerous mix of nationalism and patriotism that is hostile toward the West. In this scenario, Russian nationalists in Russia and elsewhere have taken to the streets in violent protests of Putin's inability to resolve the Ukraine crisis decisively in Russia's favor and to save the deteriorating Russian economy. One demonstration in Latvia has resulted in the accidental shooting of a Russian protest leader by a Latvian Police Officer – raw video footage of the incident has gone viral online. Protesters demand that Putin live up to his pledge as protector of Russia and take stronger actions in Ukraine and the region. Some of the most vocal nationalist leaders and media have even called for a new government.

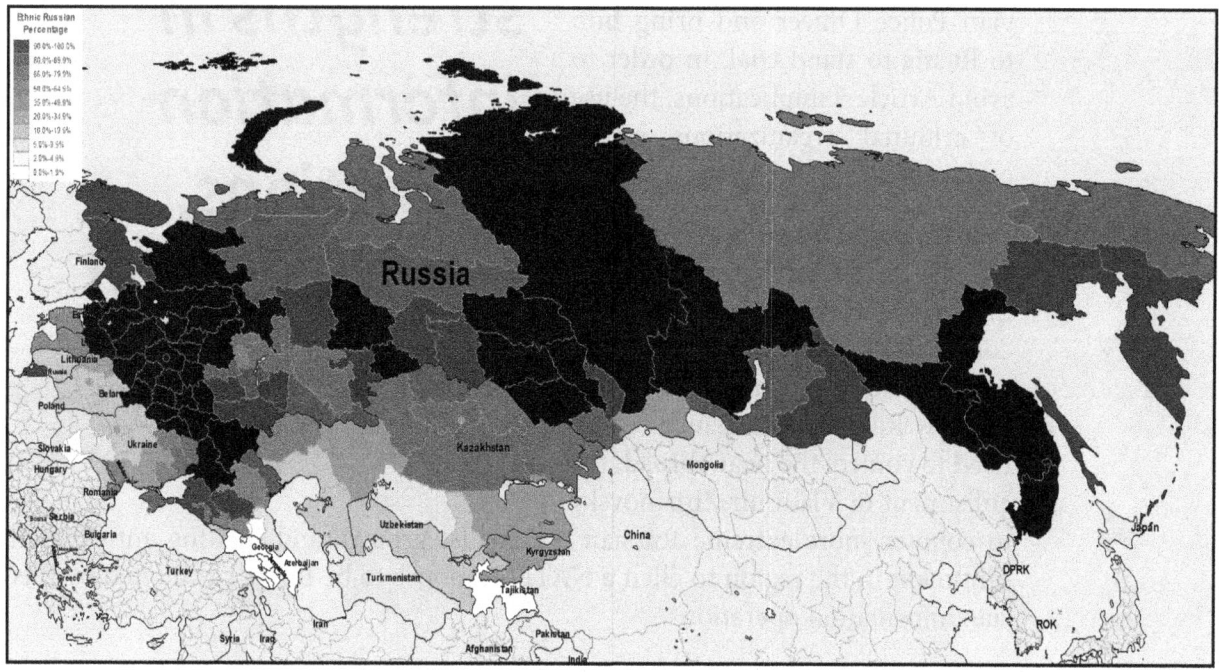

Figure 3: Ethnic Russian Population

The Russia Team assessed that Moscow's primary challenge would be demonstrating strength to the Russian people without provoking a wider conflict with NATO. Putin in particular would likely feel compelled to take action or face losing legitimacy in the eyes of the Russian people. Other Russia Team assessments included the following:

- It seems likely that Moscow would deploy military forces within a few kilometers of the Russia-Latvia border. Blending information and influence operations throughout such moves, Moscow would likely characterize any deployments as purely defensive. Simultaneously, Moscow would likely demand an investigation into the shooting of the Russian citizen, offering to lead the investigation and any subsequent prosecution.

- Despite the rapid escalation of the crisis, Moscow would likely then try to bring about a controlled de-escalation.

- It is possible that Russia might conduct a more aggressive and clandestine operation using Russian SOF, intelligence, and transnational criminal elements to abduct the Latvian Police Officer and bring him to Russia to stand trial. In order to avoid Article 5 implications, the use of criminal organizations would create sufficient ambiguity.

Russia is likely to "rely heavily on its strengths in information operations, influence, and control."

- In any case, Russia would likely rely heavily on its strengths in information operations, influence, and control. Actions within this domain might include spinning the events to show Russian dominance of and need to control the near abroad, the enlistment of Vladimir Zhirinovsky to counter more extreme Russian nationalist groups, and inciting anti-Russian sentiment in the region to elicit a NATO response to be further exploited by Russian information operations.

- Given Russian presidential elections coming up in 2018, Putin would likely feel compelled to create some sort of "political win" in the short-term to maintain and perhaps boost his legitimacy if the Russian economy continues to struggle.

- Lastly, Russia might offer to assist the EU and the Baltic states in restoring order and creating the conditions necessary for peace. This might include a plan to contribute to a regional stability force, through which Russia could then demonstrate strength and reinforce its position as guarantor of the Russian people.

The U.S. Team assessed that Washington has an interest in supporting Russian internal stability. If so, the United States might conclude that the protests inside Russia and elsewhere, as well as the accidental shooting within Latvia, were strictly domestic issues, and that Washington would likely seek to reinforce support for democratic rules and processes.

- The United States would likely attempt to remind governments across the region about the destabilizing effects of runaway nationalism, and encourage and support actions to fully integrate ethnic and Russian-speaking populations, to include the sizeable Russian-speaking minority in Ukraine.

- Washington would also likely encourage the EU – vs. NATO – to provide border security and policing assistance to the Baltic States.

- As a means of demonstrating patience and restraint, the United States might also push to postpone planned NATO exercises near areas of tension.

- Finally, it seems likely that Washington would try to avoid reacting too aggressively – for example, by deploying U.S. or NATO forces to the Baltic States – to the deployment of any Russian forces along the Russian-Latvian border.

White Team observations reinforced the importance of restraint with two key observations:

- The NATO alliance would need to react cautiously to events in such a crisis. Sending the wrong signals to Russia could create the conditions for miscalculation as the Russians attempt paradoxically to de-escalate through escalation.

- Any U.S. effort to unilaterally escalate conflict with Russia might bring about Washington's isolation from its European allies.

In this scenario, the United States would likely struggle to compete with Russia in terms of ideas and influence. Russia would be likely to consistently exploit its advantages in the information realm and cause indecisiveness within the United States and within the West more broadly. Of special note, this scenario further highlighted the danger of differing transatlantic perspectives on regional challenges.

Turn 5: The Power Elites Turn Against Putin

The next turn of the wargame explored a possible scenario where Putin is removed from power by disaffected and disenfranchised elites. In this scenario, Putin's continued trend of centralization of control and power and his ever-shrinking inner circle has created the potential for the emergence of alternatives to Putin and an implosion of his autocracy. More specifically, in this scenario Russia's economic decline has continued with a corresponding rise in nationalist and anti-Western rhetoric from the Kremlin. However, unchecked corruption and inefficiency have continued to plague the Russian economy. Capital flight, defection of oligarchs, imprisonment of political opposition leaders, the sacking of questionable government institutional elites, the rise of strongmen like Ramzan Kadryov, and the continued consolidation of power and wealth by Putin's shrinking inner circle have created the conditions for elites across Russia to seek an alternative form of governance. Those elites, including the *siloviki*, economic oligarchs, and disaffected regional leaders have begun to seriously question the direction Putin has been setting for Russia – as a result, their self-interests have finally come into direct conflict with political loyalties. The teams considered who or what might succeed Putin, what path the new regime would set for Russia, and how the United States should approach a new Russian regime.

> *It is "unlikely that a new, fragile [post-Putin] regime would return any gains made in Crimea."*

The Russia Team assessed that it is possible that any number of radical alternatives to Putin, such as an ultra-nationalist leader, former Soviet era leaders, and progressive, liberal opposition elites, might come to power. However, the Russia Team concluded that the most likely outcome of this scenario would be a quiet *putsch* in which existing elites, perhaps led by Dmitry Medvedev, would assume control of the government and renew a program of liberalization and reform. Any new government would likely be extremely fragile and vulnerable to counteractions from other regional leaders or Moscow-based elites, and thus a follow-on regime would likely be motivated to engage in positive dialogue with the West soon after transition and power consolidation.

- The two most important priorities for the new regime would likely be to solve the Ukrainian crisis and clamp down on corruption. These efforts would buy the new regime time and space, both internationally and domestically, to establish itself and prevent Russia from slipping toward further internal conflict.

- Given the interests and motivations of the forces most likely to push Putin aside, it seems probable that a new regime would emphasize economic liberalization and perhaps even reform. Nonetheless, it would seem unlikely that a new, fragile regime would return any gains made in Crimea, or to apologize for any previous conflicts.

- If a new regime were the product of Moscow-based elites, there is the possibility for regional leaders to turn against the center. For this reason, the Russia Team assessed that a new regime would be more open to engaging with the West in order to end economic sanctions. Desperation might even push a new regime in Moscow to seek some type of economic assistance from the West, particularly if the Russian economy has entered a prolonged period of decline.

- Any new regime would be unlikely to hold power, nor win the favor of the West, without free national elections, probably within several months of coming to power.

- A new regime would likely seize the opportunity to abandon Russian isolationism and engage the West. Part of this engagement could result in a 'de-Putinization' policy which would likely be supported by the oligarchs, but with appropriate reform to prevent Russia from slipping back into the chaos of the 1990s.

The U.S. Team assessed that Putin's sudden fall from power would pose great challenges to American foreign policy while also offering the potential to fundamentally change the nature of the U.S.-Russian relationship. A cautiously optimistic Washington would therefore be likely to offer support and perhaps even assistance to a new Russian regime.

- It is likely that Washington would want to signal its willingness to engage the new regime, perhaps by lifting sanctions on the banking sector in exchange for a return to the Minsk Accords.

- Another potential tool for increased cooperation might be the reopening of mil-to-mil communications and engagement. This could have the added benefit of helping to ensure the safety and security of Russian nuclear weapons and related infrastructure.

- Nevertheless, the United States would likely remain resolute in insisting that Russia return to adhering to the rules of the international system, and that forced changes to recognized borders as well as other violations of international laws would prevent the West from fully embracing the new regime.

- Throughout, the United States would increase the odds of success if it recognized Russia's honor and treated the transition as a manifestation of self-determination within Russia.

The White Team agreed that Washington would likely be cautiously optimistic. Nonetheless, the White Team assessed that the United States would need to engage in a proactive and positive information and strategic communications campaign to take advantage of the opportunity.

- The United States would likely need to take the lead in coordination with Europe to promote positive strategic communications and influence. This would enable the West to avoid more reactive information operations, which have proven to have little impact and which may actually discredit the West.

- The West would likely need to pull any new regime in Russia into immediate discussions on European security.

- The West might increase its odds of success if it relied more upon the EU rather than NATO for engaging Russia during any transition. Germany and France, among other European nations, could be very effective in helping Russia chart a positive path for all sides during this window of change.

Turn 6: Getting Beyond Crisis Mode

In the final turn, the teams were asked to identify the ideal state of U.S.-Russia relations and to offer suggestions on how the United States and Russia might achieve this objective within five years. This scenario was designed to force proactive policy and strategy measures that each side could take outside the confines of any crisis, which had animated each of the preceding turns.

The Russia Team described Moscow's ideal state of relationship with the United States as one of mutual respect and equality. The Russia Team assessed that Russia desires global influence and the ability to participate and partner with other states in solving global problems. At the same time, Moscow also likely seeks dominance over what it considers Russia's sphere of influence, and would therefore oppose U.S. and NATO influence inside the near abroad. As long as Moscow perceives Russia to be subordinated to the U.S. and NATO, Russian foreign policy would continue to compete and counter Western actions.

> *"Russia is likely to continue pursuing dominance over Eurasia through a strong, centralized leadership system"*

- Russia is likely to continue pursuing dominance over Eurasia through a strong, centralized leadership system.

- The respect of other nations is important to the ideal state that Russia seeks for itself. Russia appears to want to participate equally within the G20 and to participate in solving crises around the globe.

- It is highly unlikely that Russia would ever tolerate the reality or perception of subordination to NATO or the United States.

- Given its insecurities, Moscow is likely to believe that treaties serve to constrain Russia and leave it little flexibility.

- Moscow is likely to favor more engagement with developing economies, in order to create an alternative to the United States and the EU as partners for development and investment.

- In the same vein, Russia is likely to accelerate efforts to improve relationships and influence within Asia.

- Russia will most likely see continuing utility in maintaining frozen conflicts as a way to ensure it can preserve its sphere of interest.

The U.S. Team assessed Russia will likely continue to frustrate Washington's vision of a Europe that is free, whole, and at peace. Hence, even though the United States may seek areas of co-operation with Russia on points of mutual interest, the best case over the next five years is a period of competitive but stable relations with Russia.

- The United States and Russia are most likely to achieve cooperation on counter terrorism, nuclear arms reductions, missile defense, space exploration, and mil-to-mil activities.

- The United States may be able to convince Russia to leave the Donbas, but it is unlikely to get Russia to return Crimea to Ukrainian authority.

- The sooner the United States accepts the new reality of a competitive relationships with Russia, the sooner the West can compete more effectively.

- The West can best promote its interests by maintaining a unified front, and by consolidating military, economic, and political strengths.

- Western strategy is likely to be more successful if NATO can more effectively compete in the contest of ideas and communication. The West should strive for information that is timely, accurate, and effectively delivered as the best means of changing the current situation of instability within Eastern Europe and thereby setting conditions for long term stability.

The White Team assessed that a primary problem for the United States in developing a long term relationship with Russia is one of size and influence. The United States has many interests around the world, but Russia's seem far more limited or concentrated. Managing this disparity will help establish the parameters for more effective long term U.S.-Russian relations.

Conclusion

Change and evolution within the strategic environment are constant. Actors, relationships, and systems adapt or transform to circumstances and events that are often very difficult to foresee. The reemergence of Russian aggression in 2014 was one such event, catching the United States and its NATO allies by surprise. The reexamination of the U.S.-Russian relationship in the past 12 months has led to a renewed search for insight into modern Russia. That search has resulted in a greater understanding of the 'Russian system' and the forces of stasis and change at work on its various components.

This project used systems thinking design methods to analyze and collaborate, leading to increased understanding of the Russian system. The subsequent wargame was tied to the design approach and led to richer levels of structured collaboration, which permitted a more in-depth analysis of Russia and U.S. policy toward Russia.

The structure of the wargame was based on scenarios and questions that Russia, the United States, and Europe will most likely face in the near to midterm. Exploring these questions shed light into how each side thought about issues, priorities, risk, and alternatives when developing policy and strategy.

Four policy considerations emerged from the wargame. The United States must:

- **Shift from a cooperative to a more competitive approach towards Russia**

- **Clearly articulate its position towards Russia, Eastern Europe, and Ukraine**

- **Challenge Russia in the competition of ideas and influence**

- **Account for the two national election cycles in 2016 and 2018**

These recommendations address specific shortcomings in the U.S. approach to Russia broadly and the crisis in Ukraine specifically. By implementing these recommendations, the United States can correct past missteps, which have collectively placed Washington in a reactive posture and contributed to misunderstanding in allied capitals as well as Moscow regarding U.S. intentions and interests.

Lightning Source UK Ltd.
Milton Keynes UK
UKOW05f2107130917
309151UK00005B/504/P

9 781329 786080